Proven Natural Ways to Lower High Blood Pressure

30 Proven Natural Superfoods To Control & Lower Your High Blood Pressure

By *Louise Jiannes*

For more great books visit:

HMWPublishing.com

Download another book for Free

I want to thank you for purchasing this book and offer you another book (just as long and valuable as this book), "Health & Fitness Mistakes You Don't Know You're Making", completely free.

Visit the link below to signup and receive it:

www.hmwpublishing.com/gift

In this book, I will break down the most common health & fitness mistakes, you are probably committing right now, and I will reveal how you can easily get in the best shape of your life!

In addition to this valuable gift, you will also have an opportunity to get our new books for free, enter giveaways, and receive other valuable emails from me. Again, visit the link to sign up:

www.hmwpublishing.com/gift

TABLE OF CONTENT

Introduction 9

Chapter 1 – Overview on High Blood Pressure 12

How Can High Blood Pressure Occur? 13

Chapter 2: The Dangers of Having High Blood Pressure 15

Damage to your Arteries 15
- Damaged and Narrowed Arteries 16
- Aneurysm 16

Damage to the Heart 17
- Coronary Artery Disease 17
- Enlarged Left Heart 17
- Heart Failure 18

Damage to the Brain 18
- Transient Ischemic Attack (TIA) 19
- Stroke 19
- Dementia 20
- Mild Cognitive Impairment 20

Damage to your kidneys 21
- Kidney Failure 21
- Kidney Scarring 22

- Kidney Artery Aneurysm 22

Chapter 3: Causes and Symptoms 23

Essential Hypertension 24

Secondary Hypertension 25

Chapter 4: Preventive Measures for High Blood Pressures 27

Preventive Factors You Can Control 27

- Maintain a Normal and Healthy Weight 28
- Eat a Balanced Diet 28
- Cut Back Sodium Consumption 29
- Limit Alcohol Intake 29
- Have a Regular Exercise 29
- Monitor Your Blood Pressure 30
- Changing your Bad Habits 30

Chapter 5: Proven Ways to Control High Blood Pressure Without Medication 32

What about if you already have that sickness in you? 32

How Can One Benefit From the Natural Treatment? .35

- Weight Loss 35
- Improved Stamina and Energy 35
- Reviving Youthfulness 36
- Controlling Hypertension 36

- No Side Effects!!! 37

Natural Ways to Control High Blood Pressure Without Medication 37

- Step #1 – Walk, walk, walk! 37
- Step #2 – Inhale, Exhale! 38
- Step #3 – Take More Potassium, Reduce Sodium in Your Diet 38
- Step #4 – Add Cocoa to Your Diet 40
- Step #5 – Alcoholic Beverage Helps, Too! 41
- Step #6 – Avoid Caffeine 41
- Step #7 – Avoid Working Too Much! 42

More Alternative Treatments to Include in Your Diet! 43

- Selenium 43
- Beta-Glucan 43
- L'Argine 44
- Fish Oil or Flaxseed 44

Chapter 6: Herb Remedies: How Can They Help to Normalize Your Blood Pressure ..46

Herbal Remedies for High Blood Pressure 46

- Arjuna (Terminalia Arjuna) 46
- Dandelion (Taraxacum Officinale) 47
- Cayenne (Capsicum Annum) 48

- Ginger (Zingiber officinale) 48
- Guggul (Commiphora Wightii) 49
- Garlic (Allium Sativum) 50
- Reishi (Ganoderma lucid) 50
- Hawthorn (Crataegus app) 51
- Hawthorn (Crataegus Laevigata) 51
- Celery (Apium Graveolens) 52
- Cocoa (Theobroma Cacao) 52
- Valerian (Valeriana Officinalis) 53
- Broccoli (Brassica Oleracea var. Italica) and Dark Leafy Greens 53
- Turmeric (Lucuma Longa) 53
- Gingko Biloba 54
- Olive Leaf Extract 54
- Jaundice Berry 54
- Cayenne 55
- Red Clover 55
- Alfalfa 56
- Parsley 56
- Gooseberry 56
- Onion and Honey 57
- Fenugreek Seed (Trigonella Foenum-Graecum) ... 57

- Lowers Blood Cholesterol 57
- Reduces Risks of Heart Disease 58
- Keeps You in Shape 58

Chapter 7: Stress Management: Empowering Mind and Body 59

The Connection Between Stress and Long-term High Blood Pressure 59

Activities that Can Reduce Blood Pressure 61

Make Your Schedule Simple 61

Be Conscious of Your Breathing 62

Do Regular Work Out 63

Meditate 64

Develop Good Sleeping Habits 65

Be Optimistic 67

Chapter 8: How Meditation Can Help in Lowering High Blood Pressure 69

Managing your Health, Saving Your Life! 72

A Way To Do Your Meditation Exercise 73

Conclusion 78

Introduction

The rising number of people affected by high blood pressure had brought awareness to the public but being aware of the sickness or its presence is not enough to exclude you from its deadly fang.

For decades, this sickness had been ignored and overlooked because of its silent symptoms which earned it the title of being the "Silent Killer" but as government's efforts are driven towards minimizing if not eliminating its presence; attention to this illness is being brought forward to the public.

If you are one of the many people, who are not comfortable living with the idea that you could be affected by this illness without actually knowing it. This book, "*Proven Natural Ways to Lower High Blood Pressure*" will equip you with the knowledge of high blood pressure and how to reverse it naturally without the use of medications.

Furthermore, while we are discussing the treatment of high blood pressure, we should also be aware of its preventive measures. Know all the essential facts about this silent killer to live a healthier life!

Also, before you get started, I recommend you **joining our email newsletter** to receive updates on any upcoming new book releases or promotions. You can sign-up for free, and as a bonus, you will receive a free gift. Our "*Health & Fitness Mistakes You Don't Know You're Making*" book! This book has been written to demystify, expose the top do's and don'ts and to finally equip you with the information you need to get in the best shape of your life. Due to the overwhelming amount of mis-information and lies told by magazines and self-proclaimed "gurus", it's becoming harder and harder to get reliable information to get in shape. As opposed to having to go through dozens of biased, unreliable and un-trustworthy sources to get your health & fitness information. Everything you need to help you has been broken down in this book for you to easily follow and to immediately get results to achieve your desired fitness goals in the shortest amount of time.

Once again, to join our free email newsletter and to receive a free copy of this valuable book, please visit the link and signup now:

www.hmwpublishing.com/gift

Chapter 1 – Overview on High Blood Pressure

High blood pressure is one of the primary contributing causes of death in the United States. According to the recent report released by the Center for Disease and Control Prevention, about 75 million American adults have high blood pressure. To give you a quick calculation, that's one out of every three adult Americans or around 29% of the American population. Approximately $46 billion is spent by the nation each year to cover health care services and medications. This also includes missed days of work due to hypertension.

Symptoms of high blood pressure are sometimes so mild that it's hard to detect. However, its results can be deadly and therefore must be taken with the utmost concern. Untreated, high blood pressure, also known as "hypertension can damage and can leave scars to the arteries which can also be found even in people who are normally calm and relaxed. The "Silent Killer," as it carries no initial symptoms, is a long-term illness, which can eventually lead to complications and death.

HOW CAN HIGH BLOOD PRESSURE OCCUR?

High blood pressure is the impact of the blood created against the wall of the arteries as it circulates inside the human body. The blood pressure is determined by the amount of blood pumped by the heart against its resistance as it flows through the arteries.

When there are some blockades like cholesterol build up, scarring or plaque in the arteries, it affects the elasticity of the arterial walls and narrows the way of the bloodstream, thereby creating more pressure as the heart pumps harder to get the blood through so that it can reach the different parts of the body. Such increase in pressure can damage the muscles and valves of the heart and may result in heart failure. Damages to the vessels supplying blood and oxygen to kidneys and brain eventually create a negative impact on these body organs.

Too much pressure in the blood vessels and arterial walls can cause serious problems. Healthy arteries are usually semi-flexible tissues and muscles that are fine, smooth, elastic and stretchable, so blood flows smoothly through them when the heart starts to pump mildly. However, when there are blockades, the heart is forced to pump more thereby stretching the walls of the arteries, and if done too much, it could break the lining of the arterial walling. Once blood vessels are broken, it could lead to stroke, kidneys malfunction, peripheral vascular failure or heart attack, which causes death to the majority of its victims.

It is, therefore, essential to keep your blood pressure at a level to reduce the risk of blood vessels from getting overstretch beyond its limit. Uncontrolled blood pressure increases the risk of more serious health or medical problems to occur.

Chapter 2: The Dangers of Having High Blood Pressure

High blood pressure is steadily increasing in modern societies due to an unhealthy lifestyle. This can be very disturbing if you are not fully aware of its implications in your health condition, but if you do, you can look for useful options to reverse its effects.

High blood pressure can silently do some serious damage to your body system long before the onset of symptoms. Taking it for granted can result to a disability, a life of suffering, and even a severe heart attack. People who are left untreated of high blood pressure die of ischemic heart disease or reduced blood flow. Others die of stroke. A shift in lifestyle and treatment can help control your high blood pressure to reduce these life-threatening risks. Now, let's take a look to some of the damages it can cause to your body.

Damage to your Arteries

When your arteries are healthy, they are flexible, elastic, and strong with a smooth inner lining along the walls to let the blood flow freely as it circulates the body. This is a vital process as it supplies nutrients and oxygen to vital tissues and organs. When the bloodstream is clogged, it causes an increase in pressure in the arterial wall as the heart pumps vigorously to let the blood flow in. As a result, you could be experiencing the following:

- *DAMAGED AND NARROWED ARTERIES*

    When you have an unhealthy lifestyle, your body can collect fats from your diet and store them in your arteries, clogging the flow of the bloodstream and your artery walls become less elastic. This limits the flow of blood in your body.

- *ANEURYSM*

    Eventually, the constant pressure of blood against the weakened artery lining may cause a part of the wall to form a bulge. This condition is called "an aneurysm." An aneurysm can rupture anytime and can cause internal bleeding in any of your arteries, but mostly it occurs in the aorta or the largest artery in your body.

DAMAGE TO THE HEART

Since your heart pumps blood to your body, uncontrolled high blood pressure can do damage to your heart in many ways.

- *CORONARY ARTERY DISEASE*

    This condition affects the arteries that supply blood to the body. The disease narrows down the arteries and limits the blood to flow freely through the arteries. When you have this illness, you can experience irregular heart rhythms known as (arrhythmias), chest pains or an irregular heart attack.

- *ENLARGED LEFT HEART*

    When your heart is forced to exert vigorously to pump blood into your body, it causes the left ventricle to become stiffen or thickens (left ventricular hypertrophy). These changes also limit the ventricle's ability to pump blood thereby increasing the risk of a heart failure, heart, attack and sudden cardiac death.

- *HEART FAILURE*

    Eventually, the strain on your heart caused by the high blood pressure weakens your heart muscles and makes them work less efficiently. If this continues to go on, this condition will just wear out your heart. Your heart will wear out in time and fail and if there's some damage caused by heart attack, they add more to the existing problem.

DAMAGE TO THE BRAIN

Like your heart, the brain depends on the supply of blood to nourish it so it can work properly to survive. However, when there is high blood pressure, it can cause problems including what we have here below.

- *TRANSIENT ISCHEMIC ATTACK (TIA)*

   Considered as a "mini-stroke," this condition is a temporary disruption of the blood supply to your brain. Transient Ischemic Condition is often caused by atherosclerosis or a blood clot. Both of these can arise when there is high blood pressure, and the presence of the TIA is a warning that you're at risk for a full-blown stroke.

- *STROKE*

   When part of your brain is deprived of oxygen and nutrients supplied by your blood vessels, it will cause the death of your brain cells. So, when you have high blood pressure that is left uncontrolled or neglected, this can cause the narrowing, rupture or leaks in your blood vessels leading to the brain. High blood pressure can likewise cause blood clotting in the arteries blocking the blood flow to your brain and causing a stroke.

- *DEMENTIA*

    This condition is associated with problems in cognitive abilities – thinking, speaking, reasoning, memory, vision, and movements. There are various causes of dementia including vascular dementia, which is attained through narrowing and blockage of the arteries that supply blood to the brain. It can also result in a stroke that causes an interruption in the blood flow leading to the brain. In any of these cases, it's the high blood pressure that mainly causes it.

- *MILD COGNITIVE IMPAIRMENT*

    There is a transition stage, which occurs between the changes in understanding, and memory as one grows old and the more severe problems develop when one gets, for example, an Alzheimer's disease. Like dementia, this results from blocked blood flow when high blood pressure damages arteries.

DAMAGE TO YOUR KIDNEYS

Typically, it's the function of your kidneys to filter excess waste and fluids from your blood, though this process depends on your healthy blood vessels. When high blood pressure injures your blood vessels leading to your kidneys, it may cause numerous types of kidney diseases (nephropathy). If you have diabetes, this can even worsen the damage.

- *KIDNEY FAILURE*

    Kidney failure is caused by high blood pressure as it brings damage both to the large arteries leading to your kidneys and the tiny blood vessels (glomeruli) within the kidneys. Damage to either of these two affects the normal function of your kidneys hindering it from efficiently filtering waste from the blood. In the end, a dangerous level of waste and fluids can accumulate in your body and may ultimately require dialysis or a kidney transplant.

- *KIDNEY SCARRING*

  Glomerulosclerosis is a type of kidney damage caused by scarring of the glomeruli (glue-MER-u-li). The glomeruli are tiny clusters of blood vessels within your kidneys that filter fluid and waste from your blood. Glomerulosclerosis can leave your kidneys unable to filter waste efficiently, leading to kidney failure.

- *KIDNEY ARTERY ANEURYSM*

  This is a type of an aneurysm leading to the kidney. One potential cause of this disease is atherosclerosis, which damages and weakens the artery wall. In the long run, a weakened artery can cause a section to form an aneurysm, which can rupture anytime and cause a life threatening internal bleeding.

CHAPTER 3: CAUSES AND SYMPTOMS

It's not easy to identify the exact cause of high blood pressure, but numerous factors and conditions that may somehow have contributed to its development.

Here are some among them:

- Obesity or overweight

- Lack of physical activity

- Too much consumption of salt and alcohol

- Smoking

- Genes and family history including high blood pressure

- Unmanageable stress

- Chronic kidney ailments

- Thyroid and adrenal disorders

- Sleep apnea

ESSENTIAL HYPERTENSION

In the United States, more than 95% of reported high blood pressure cases, the underlying cause is not determined. For this type of high blood pressure, people in the medical world call it as the "essential hypertension."

Mysterious as it is, essential hypertension has been linked to specific risk factors. High blood pressure tends to affect more males than their female counterparts and is likewise observed to run in the family.

Moreover, age and race also play a vital role. African Americans living in the United States are twice as more likely to have high blood pressure compared to Caucasians, but the gap decreases at around age 44. Many black women have the highest reported incidence of high blood pressure at the age of 65 and above.

Other factors that affect essential hypertension are diet and lifestyle. The link between salt and high blood pressure has long been established. Japanese people living in the northern islands of Japan are known to consume more salt per capita than people in the rest of the world, and they've got the highest incidence of essential hypertension. Conversationally, who don't use salt to their food have no traces of essential hypertension.

People with high blood pressure are hypersensitive, in other words, this means that even a small excess of salt added to what is typically needed by the body can send their blood pressure to soar up. Other factors that count in the presence of essential high blood pressure are an insufficiency in calcium, magnesium, and potassium, chronic alcohol consumption, obesity, and diabetes.

SECONDARY HYPERTENSION

Contrary to essential high blood pressure is the Secondary High Blood Pressure or "secondary hypertension." This type of high blood pressure, the direct cause is somehow pinpointed, and kidney disease ranks the highest among the many causes of secondary hypertension.

This type of high blood pressure can be triggered by tumors and other abnormalities, which cause the adrenal glands to produce excess amounts of hormones that elevate the blood pressure.

The factors that can send blood pressure to rise include:

- Pregnancy

- Birth control pills particularly those that contain estrogen

- Drugs that constrict blood vessels

Chapter 4: Preventive Measures for High Blood Pressures

Making an extra effort to prevent the onset of high blood pressure can help in the reduction of stroke, heart attack, and many other serious illnesses that can lead to death. If you are at risk for high blood pressure, it's best for you to take these preventive measures.

Preventive Factors You Can Control

Some factors like, age and genes including family medical histories are elements that are beyond your control. Therefore, if you want to prevent the onset of high blood pressure, you need to focus on the risk factors that you can change. We are not able to do something about our age or what constitutes our DNA, but we can always change our lifestyle for a better and healthy one.

Here are some ways to consider in shifting to a healthy lifestyle.

- *MAINTAIN A NORMAL AND HEALTHY WEIGHT*

    Maintaining a healthy weight is crucial when it comes to hypertension. Overweight and obesity can lead to more complications, which can eventually lead to death. People who are overweight need to lose weight and if you are of average weight, then avoid adding more pounds. Finally, if you are carrying extra weight, lose as much as ten pounds to help prevent the occurrence of high blood pressure. There are online resources to help you know your ideal weight and your body mass index (BMI).

- *EAT A BALANCED DIET*

    Eating a healthy balanced diet can help keep your blood pressure under control. Eat foods that are rich in potassium while keeping a limit on calories, fat, sodium, and sugar. DASH Diet is known to help in managing high blood pressure.

- **CUT BACK SODIUM CONSUMPTION**

    The higher the sodium intake you have, the higher the blood pressure rises. Therefore, it is better to cut down on your sodium intake by avoiding foods that are high in sodium content like packaged foods and processed food. It may also help to prevent adding salt to your meals.

- **LIMIT ALCOHOL INTAKE**

    Drinking too much alcohol thickens the blood and therefore creates more pressure for the heart to have it flowed smoothly and freely. Thus, avoid having more than a drink in a day.

- **HAVE A REGULAR EXERCISE**

    It takes activity to make one healthy, and physical activity is crucial when referring to high blood pressure. The more exercise you have, the better. However, even a little bit of exercise can do so much to lessen the risk of hypertension. Start doing a moderate amount of exercise for about 30 minutes. Starting by training two to three times a week is an ideal target to begin.

- *MONITOR YOUR BLOOD PRESSURE*

    After you have done with the ways stated above, make sure that you regularly monitor your blood pressure. To do this, you can either go to a clinic or do this at home. Since hypertension often shows no apparent symptoms, only the blood pressure reading can give you a definite measurement of your blood pressure. Blood pressure reading in the range of 120-139/80-89 millimeters of mercury (mmHg) puts you at an increased risk of developing high blood pressure.

- *CHANGING YOUR BAD HABITS*

    Finally, take a look at your lifestyle and see what among your habits needs to change. Try conquering small goals like eating fruits and vegetables instead of junk foods in between meals. Make these habits as part of your daily routine.

Chapter 5: Proven Ways to Control High Blood Pressure Without Medication

Although we have introduced some preventive measures to get away from having high blood pressure, still we know it is not that easy to make a 360 degrees shift in your lifestyle. With the kind of modern life we have today, when almost everyone is always on the go, we fill in our stomachs with ready-to-eat foods right out of the package. We know that these foods are far from being healthy and unless you are determined to change your ways, you need to refrain from eating theses kind of foods.

What about if you already have that sickness in you?

As I have stated, high blood pressure is a sickness that must not be ignored. Deaths related to high blood pressure run to almost 100,000 each year and is still rapidly increasing.

Some people just ignore their problem while others choose medications with harmful effects. But, nowadays, the majority of people resort back to the use of simple natural remedies to treat high blood pressure. There are many natural remedies proven over the years to combat high blood pressure.

Before considering drug medication for your hypertension problem, take note of the following facts:

- ✓ Pharmaceutical companies are considered to be one of the most lucrative businesses in the 21st Century.

- ✓ The number of hospitals has grown these past decades exponentially. Before it was believed to be due to baby boomers or those in their retirement age, however, recent studies are showing that people tend to rely more on doctors nowadays for every aspect of their physical health.

- ✓ Insurance rates and coverage have grown too high partly due to inflated medical and prescriptions cost.

Obviously, not all drugs are dangerous. Many have their purpose in life are beneficial to our society. However, some drugs are harmful in some ways as they are harsh and carry deadly side effects in many ways.

Nonetheless, millions of people are still choosing to forego using medications with dangerous side effects and instead resort to the holistic and natural treatment of high blood pressure. With holistic treatment, we refer to the kind of healing that view the wholeness of a person. That is, instead of focusing on the treatment of a disease, the holistic approach looks at an individual's overall physical, emotional, mental, and spiritual well being before recommending treatment.

This holistic approach to natural treatment might involve a nutritional diet, regular exercise, meditation, and much more. Attacking high blood pressure on many different angles can completely cure the person without the use of drug medication!

How Can One Benefit From the Natural Treatment?

Beside from the avoidance of the life-threatening side effects of drugs, there are various reasons why you need to consider treating high blood pressure naturally.

Here are some things you should consider doing:

- *WEIGHT LOSS*

    People who undergo natural treatments learn not only how they are cured of their high blood pressure, but also managed to shed extra pounds. When you know the right kind of food to eat, you will minimize your cravings and therefore can lose 1-2 pounds in a week.

- *IMPROVED STAMINA AND ENERGY*

    Because of proper nutrition, you will experience improved stamina and energy and therefore can do things that you can enjoy. When one has a healthy body, life can be better compared to those who don't have a healthy and fit body.

- *REVIVING YOUTHFULNESS*

    When you have high blood pressure, you are missing out on significant vitamins and minerals that are needed by the body. Vitamins and minerals like calcium, magnesium, and zinc play a vital role in normalizing your blood pressure. When you have adequate of these substances, then you will feel much younger and alive.

- *CONTROLLING HYPERTENSION*

    There are over a thousand listed benefits for exercising and controlling your blood pressure is one of them. Learn a simple exercise, which you can do every day for 20-30 minutes, and you will eventually experience that your blood pressure is going back to normal.

- *NO SIDE EFFECTS!!!*

    Unlike medicine drugs, the only side effect you can get from taking natural remedy is feeling bad about not trying it sooner.

NATURAL WAYS TO CONTROL HIGH BLOOD PRESSURE WITHOUT MEDICATION

Changing lifestyle is said to show a normalized blood pressure in around 86 percent of those who have this disease. Therefore, if you want to reverse your hypertension, you need to normalize your weight. Once you begin to have healthier eating habits, then you can start adapting to the following strategies to beat your hypertension.

- *STEP #1 – WALK, WALK, WALK!*

    Start to walk as much as you can. Work up to walk slowly for longer and longer distances. Try power walking – brisk walking for about 30 minutes a day. This activity can increase your oxygen supply in the body to keep your heart function smoothly and efficiently. As you get used to power walking, try to increase your speed and distance while you increase strength and stamina.

- *STEP #2 – INHALE, EXHALE!*

   Take time to breathe deeply. Sit in a chair with your back straight. Breathe as deeply as you can for five or ten minutes. Stress hormones elevate a kidney enzyme called renin, which raises blood pressure. By slowly deep breathing and expanding your belly, you exhale all the tension out of your body. Adding qigong, tai chi, meditation or yoga to that deep breath is another excellent stress buster.

- *STEP #3 – TAKE MORE POTASSIUM, REDUCE SODIUM IN YOUR DIET*

   Watch out for the amount of animal protein in your diet because overeating some of it causes a rise in your body acid levels and diminishes your potassium level. Therefore, it is better to add more naturally potassium-rich foods to your meals such as fresh fruits and vegetables, whole grain, dairy and poultry products, meat, and fish.

High potassium-rich foods include broccoli, halibut, tuna, spinach, parsley, oranges, bananas, avocados, strawberries, crimini mushrooms, Brussels sprouts, kidney beans, tuna, eggplant, apricots, dried prunes, raisins, cantaloupe, honeydew melon, potatoes, peas, squash, chard, sweet potatoes, bell peppers, cucumbers, tomatoes, and cabbage.

Buy as little processed food and limit your sodium intake by buying food that contains a higher level of sodium. You can avoid this by reading food labels, as you will become more aware of the amount of salt in every pack of food that you buy in the grocery store or supermarket.

People with high blood pressure are sometimes salt-sensitive. Because there is no available test to show if you are sensitive to salt or not, it is, therefore, essential to be aware of how much salt you are taking so to be able to reduce as much as possible.

- *STEP #4 – ADD COCOA TO YOUR DIET*

    A half an ounce of dark chocolate added to your diet contains at least 70 percent cocoa. Dark chocolate contains a substance called "flavanols", which make blood vessel more elastic. The elasticity of blood vessels helps to lower down high blood pressure.

    Cocoa flavanols are bioactive derived from cacao beans. Studies on cacao beans disclosed that flavanols could improve cardiovascular functions while lowering the burden on the heart that comes along with aging and heart's stiffening. The study further reveals that the intake of cocoa flavanols reduces the risk of developing cardiovascular diseases.

- *STEP #5 – ALCOHOLIC BEVERAGE HELPS, TOO!*

    Having about ¼ -1/2 drink of alcoholic beverage helps to lower your blood pressure. Studies revealed that a small amount of alcoholic drink in a day decreases the risk of heart disease and protects the heart. However, more than that is sure to be detrimental.

- *STEP #6 – AVOID CAFFEINE*

    Studies about caffeine show that it causes high blood pressure by tightening blood vessels. This highlights the effects of stress and raises high blood pressure as well. Therefore, you can avoid a blood pressure spikes when you are stressed by using decaf coffee and other drinks.

Drinking hibiscus coffee is associated with a significant decrease in hypertension. A study has proven that drinking 3 cups of hibiscus coffee a day for six weeks brings a substantial change in the level of blood pressure of participants. The Journal of Nutrition had published that hibiscus tea can cause the blood pressure to lower down naturally and was effective in adults who are classified as either mildly hypertensive or pre-hypertensive.

- *STEP #7 – AVOID WORKING TOO MUCH!*

    Working for more than 41 hours in a week can add hypertension to the list of health risks since people who works too much tend to eat less healthy food and do not have enough time to exercise. Overload of responsibilities and tasks adds stress to your daily routine, which could later bring you more health issues. Therefore, try to rest as often as you can.

MORE ALTERNATIVE TREATMENTS TO INCLUDE IN YOUR DIET!

There are many other ways to normalize your high blood pressure, and you can include these in your diet. Here are some of them.

- ### SELENIUM

    Selenium, copper, and zinc are just some of the compound elements that can be helpful. Many studies show how people with heart diseases are often deficient of these items. You can have supplements some of these features by taking multi-vitamins in your diet. Sources of selenium are meat, walnuts, Brazil nuts, dark greens, and wheat. Zinc is usually found in beans, meat, and dairy while copper is present in seafood, legumes, nuts, and dark, leafy vegetables.

- ### BETA-GLUCAN

    This substance lowers cholesterol level and likewise reduces blood pressure resulting from high cholesterol.

You can get beta-glucan from oat bran and maitake mushroom. This element further aids in moving waste materials out of the human body. A 200-milligram of oat bran (about a teaspoon) to be taken daily can lower hypertension.

- *L'ARGINE*

By taking 2 grams of L'argine a day can reduce systolic pressure by 20 points after you have taken the supplement for two days. It is primariy due to the amino acid that helps the body to produce nitric acid, which regulates blood pressure and cholesterol.

- *FISH OIL OR FLAXSEED*

Known as Omega 3 fatty acid, fish oil is beneficial for those who are suffering from hypertension. Fish oil protects the heart as well as lowers the blood pressure. For vegetarians, you can try flaxseed. Consuming just a tablespoon of the flaxseed daily can help you lower down your hypertension by nine points.

Chapter 6: Herb Remedies: How Can They Help to Normalize Your Blood Pressure

One of the naturally accepted treatments for high blood pressure is the use of herbal as home remedies. The recent increase in the movement away from drug medication is mainly because of the fact that people are fed up with the side effects resulting from the use of drug medication, not to say the costly prescriptions.

Herbal Remedies for High Blood Pressure

- *Arjuna (Terminalia Arjuna)*

    The Arjuna plant is associated with high blood pressure treatment. Its bark is known for its remarkable remedy of the sickness by protecting the heart and stopping the bleeding as well as toughening the muscles in the organ while improving the blood circulation.

Triterpene Glycosides and *Coenzymes Q10* compound substances that help the heart and the arterial blood vessels to function properly are said to be abundant in Arjuna plant. Regular use of this herbal medicine will help eliminate the risk of hypertension and prevent further damage to the heart and the rest of vital organs that are affected by high blood pressure.

- DANDELION *(TARAXACUM OFFICINALE)*

If you have an issue on fluid retention, dandelion can be useful as it helps increase the urine flow and helps lower blood pressure. One can benefit from the use of dandelions through the elimination of potassium loss, which pharmaceutical diuretics often have. However, make sure that when you use these dandelion leaves, they are not treated with pesticides.

- *CAYENNE (CAPSICUM ANNUM)*

    Cayenne aids in thinning of the blood, thus lowering your blood pressure. Just use the hot Mexican or Thai seeds like those used in Serrano or African Bird Peppers, which are among the hottest of the cayenne products.

    To use cayenne for remedy, just take a cup of lukewarm water mixed with one teaspoon of cayenne pepper. Drink the solution for maintenance.

- *GINGER (ZINGIBER OFFICINALE)*

    Another herb that is commonly used as a cooking spice is ginger. Though we often consume this home kitchen ingredient, yet most are not aware of its health benefits, including regulating high blood pressure. Ginger is very useful in improving blood flow, treating nausea, relaxing muscles of the arteries, facilitating easy digestion, and easing morning sickness.

Garlic may come in various forms including dry roots, capsules, fresh roots, oils, liquid extracts, powders, supplements, etc. You can eat garlic raw or add it to your delectable dishes.

While ginger is proclaimed as safe and effective for hypertension, some people may experience some possible side effects which you must be cautious of – Allergic reactions, gastric disturbance, heartburn problems or mouth irritation.

- *GUGGUL (COMMIPHORA WIGHTII)*

  Primarily, this herb grows in India but can also be found in other countries in Central Asia and Northern Africa. Studies indicate that this amazing herb can reduce bad cholesterol LDL and likewise address health issues related to psoriasis, arteriosclerotic vascular disease, and cardiac ischemia.

- *GARLIC (ALLIUM SATIVUM)*

For a long time, we have recognized garlic as an aromatic ingredient we used for food seasoning. However, we failed to realize that garlic lowers down our blood pressure by ten percent. Even when it's in the form of gel capsules, garlic still has the same effect.

Garlic also possesses the capability to lessen blood clotting and clears your arteries of bad cholesterols and plaques. For better performance, daily consumption of 1 or 2 cloves for 90 days is enough to prevent and minimize the effects of high blood pressure. It can either be eaten raw or included in your meals.

- *REISHI (GANODERMA LUCID)*

This is one species of mushroom associated with lowering of blood pressure. The mushroom is almost inedible but available in capsule form.

- *HAWTHORN (CRATAEGUS APP)*

  Hawthorn causes arterial walls to relax and dilate, and it can take many weeks or months to show any effect.

- *HAWTHORN (CRATAEGUS LAEVIGATA)*

  Hawthorn is beneficial in widening arterial blood vessels, preventing the growth of atherosclerosis, decreasing cholesterol levels, enhancing blood circulation, and regulating heartbeat.

You can consume this herb by drinking it in tea form using its dried leaves and flowers. You may also include hawthorn berry supplements in your dietary plan. Whatever way you use, you can experience a 2.60 HG reduction in your blood pressure level. All these results established hawthorn as a highly trusted herbal treatment for blood pressure.

- *CELERY (APIUM GRAVEOLENS)*

Celery has been used as a remedy since the early age, and it occupies a unique herbal treatment for blood pressure. It aids in increasing the flow of urine. Indians have used it in their daily life having recognized celery as one of the best remedies for high blood pressure.

- *COCOA (THEOBROMA CACAO)*

Another fantastic herb that is associated with lowering high blood pressure efficiently is the Cocoa. It works as antioxidants like tea and red wine. According to researchers, a daily dose of 3.5 ounces of cocoa is effective as taking a daily dose of high blood pressure medication.

- *VALERIAN (VALERIANA OFFICINALIS)*

    Valerian relaxes the smooth muscles lining the arterial walls by preventing them from constricting.

- *BROCCOLI (BRASSICA OLERACEA VAR. ITALICA) AND DARK LEAFY GREENS*

    Broccoli and dark leafy vegetables are high in vitamins and minerals that are an essential need for people with high blood pressure. Magnesium and calcium are found in abundance in broccoli and other dark leafy vegetables.

- *TURMERIC (LUCUMA LONGA)*

    Turmeric, the spice, is often used in curries. It has anti-inflammatory and antioxidant properties that lower cholesterol level and strengthen body vessels as well as reduce blood pressure.

- ***GINGKO BILOBA***

    Gingko Biloba is known Chinese herbal remedy for hypertension that improves circulation of the blood and dilates arteries. It also enhances memory and makes one mentally alert.

- ***OLIVE LEAF EXTRACT***

    The extract derived from the olive leaf is used as a remedy for high blood pressure to combat irregular heartbeat or what is called "arrhythmia."

- ***JAUNDICE BERRY***

    With this herbal remedy, blood flow is facilitated to run smoothly in the arteries by dilating blood vessels through the release of tension on the arteries.

- **CAYENNE**

    Cayenne is known as the best herb for high blood pressure next to garlic. To get the best results, choose the hottest of the cayenne spices. Cayenne is known to result in proper control of blood pressure.

- **RED CLOVER**

    People with high blood pressure tend to have their blood thickened resulting to the extra effort of the heart in pumping blood through the vessels. The pressure therefore against the arteries is heightened causing hypertension. Red clover is best for thinning blood hence, lowering blood pressure, and improving blood circulation. To be efficiently used, the red clover needs to be in good state – blossoms must remain purple. Brown coloured clover is dry and has lost their effectiveness.

- *ALFALFA*

    Alfalfa helps in softening hardened arteries while reducing high blood pressure. It plays a vital role in hypertension treatment.

- *PARSLEY*

    Parsley is best in maintaining blood circulation and the whole circulatory system of the body while it lowers high blood pressure.

- *GOOSEBERRY*

    Known as "Amla" in India, gooseberry can be consumed with honey in its juice form. Take 1-2 tablespoon daily on an empty stomach as is a primarily beneficial to people with high blood pressure.

- *ONION AND HONEY*

    A mixture of onion juice and honey can do wonders for people with high blood pressure. Drinking two teaspoons a day of this mixture can reverse the effect of high blood pressure and helps you return to a stable blood pressure.

- *FENUGREEK SEED (TRIGONELLA FOENUM-GRAECUM)*

    Seeds from this plant are known to carry various health benefits <u>including the following:</u>

- LOWERS BLOOD CHOLESTEROL

    Studies have proven that fenugreek helps in reducing cholesterol level, particularly that of LDL or low-density lipoprotein. The herb is known to be enriched with steroidal saponins, which is associated with the absorption of cholesterol and triglycerides.

- **REDUCES RISKS OF HEART DISEASE**

    Fenugreek leaves contain a high amount of potassium that counters the adverse effects of sodium in the body to help control heartbeat rate and blood pressure.

- **KEEPS YOU IN SHAPE**

    When you include fenugreek in your diet by chewing soaked seeds in the morning on an empty stomach, the natural fiber in the fenugreek can fill up and causes your stomach to swell, suppressing your appetite. This aids you in attaining your weight loss goals, as you also tend to lose your cravings for foods.

All the above conditions are beneficial and will help you naturally lower your high blood pressure.

Chapter 7: Stress Management: Empowering Mind and Body

It's still debatable whether long-term blood pressure and stress are connected. However, taking measures to manage and reduce your stress dramatically benefits your overall health including your blood pressure.

The Connection Between Stress and Long-term High Blood Pressure

While experts cannot define the direct relationship between these two, it's proven that stressful events can cause temporary increase in blood pressure. What you can do to avoid long-term high blood pressure is to take preventive measures that will benefit your health in both mind and body.

Exercising is a drug-free way of helping you lower your blood pressure. It reduces your stress levels as it releases endorphins, which are essential in making you feel good about yourself and the things around you. For instance, you can exercise 3-5 times a week for about half an hour to reduce your stress level. Other physical activities such as doing household chores, gardening, dancing, swimming, or jogging can also increase your breathing and heart rates, generating benefits in rendering your blood pressure under control.

Remember that under stressful situations, your body produces a rush of hormones, which can cause your heart to beat faster for a while and narrowing your blood vessels in the process. As we mentioned earlier, there's no absolute proof that stress directly results in long-term blood pressure but behaviours such as overeating, smoking, substance abuse and observing poor sleeping habits can all contribute to high blood pressure. Overtime, these series of temporary sharp increases in blood pressure can put you in danger of having a long-term high blood pressure.

On the other hand, stress-related health conditions such as isolation, anxiety, and depression, which can be connected to heart disease may not be related to high blood pressure at all. The reason may be because of the hormones that are produced during the stressful moments.

These hormones can then damage the arteries, exposing you to the risks of heart disease. Additionally, if you are stressed or depressed, you also tend to neglect yourself. This includes the probability of not taking necessary medications that can control your high blood pressure and heart condition.

ACTIVITIES THAT CAN REDUCE BLOOD PRESSURE

Stress management is a skill that can help you in a lot of ways. Mastering it can help you live a healthy lifestyle that can benefit your overall health—both mind and boy—including the regulation of your blood pressure. The following steps may help you get started in how to handle your stress:

MAKE YOUR SCHEDULE SIMPLE

One of the most challenging things most of us experience is how to simplify our schedule. Usually, we tend to procrastinate only to find ourselves in a rush to finish our work, projects, assignments, etc. With this hustle and bustle, it's quite reasonable that our body accepts this as stress, which isn't good for our body when accumulated over time.

Eliminate or curtail additional activities that take up a lot of your time. For example, chatting with your friends on Facebook takes a great deal of your morning schedule. Instead of doing this, you can choose a more time-worthy activity wherein you can move around your body or exercise your mind, such as trying to meditate.

BE CONSCIOUS OF YOUR BREATHING

Breathing is essential for us; after all, we breathe to live. When we breathe, each cell in our body takes in the supply of oxygen that contributes to the production of energy in our system. It also allows us to get rid of the toxins that our body must eliminate to stay healthy.

Unfortunately, most of us take breathing for granted. Busy schedule and fast-paced lifestyle contribute more to our neglect in taking deep breaths which are very important in our health.

You can do simple breathing exercises by doing deep inhalation and exhalation all throughout the day. Take a few deep breaths and let your body relax, letting go of the stressors accumulating in your body. This process allows you to intake oxygen and feeds the cells of your body the much-needed supply necessary for your survival.

Do Regular Work Out

In this modern age wherein computers and various gadgets dominate our lifestyle, we tend to be sedentary. Remember that physical activity is a natural stress reliever. With the advice of your doctor, you can plan your exercises starting from simple activities such as walking or jogging. You can also try these various activities:

- Doing household chores and gardening
- Climbing the stairs
- Walking (in the park or any relaxing place)

- Dancing
- Playing tennis, basketball, or dodgeball

MEDITATE

Meditation has been proven to benefit the health of both our mind and body. It helps us to relax and have that inner calm that is essential to achieving balance.

Back in 2008, Massachusetts General Hospital doctor Randy Zusman asked his patients with high blood pressure to undertake a three-month-long meditation-base relaxation program. These patients regularly took medication to control their high blood pressure. After three months, 40 out of 60 patients displayed a remarkable drop in their blood pressure levels.

As a result, they were able to lessen their medication intake. The scientific explanation about this is that as the body and mind enter the state of relaxation, nitric oxide can then be formed resulting in the opening of blood vessels, regulating the flow of blood pressure.

Yoga helps you to control your blood pressure. In doing regular stretches, your muscles can become flexible resulting in controlled blood pressure without the use of medications. Stretching exercises develop a series of physiological reactions that may inhibit the stiffening of arteries due to aging.

DEVELOP GOOD SLEEPING HABITS

When you are deprived of sleep, you usually gain weight due to the lowering of your *leptin* (the hormone in charge of prompting your brain that you already had enough food eaten) hormone levels and an increase of the biochemical called *ghrelin* which intensifies your appetite to eat.

This bodily reaction dramatically affects your eating behavior, making you intake high amounts of calories which your body doesn't need.

Additionally, sleep deprivation also makes your body release higher levels of insulin after you eat, boosting fat storage and exposing you to a higher risk of having type-2 diabetes.

Sleep plays a vital role in repairing and healing your blood vessels as well as your heart. Lack of it promotes high blood pressure, stroke and heart disease.

According to one study of Harvard Medical School, patients with high blood pressure may experience the hike of their blood pressure levels all throughout the next day upon staying late the night before. To help yourself fight off sleep deprivation, here are the best steps that you should observe:

- Consume caffeine only in mornings.
- Set aside your mobile devices and other gadgets after dinner.
- Observe a consistent wake-up schedule.
- Avoid using sedatives like Valium, Nyquil, Ambien or even alcohol.
- Take a 15-minute nap every afternoon instead of drinking coffee.

BE OPTIMISTIC

Having a positive mindset and attitude dramatically helps in promoting your overall health. When you're mind is relaxed, your body automatically creates balance and harmony leading to good health—and regulating your blood pressure levels is one of the benefits of having this inner calm. Quite some studies also show that being optimistic tend to give a person a quality and long life. For instance, a happy and contented person who enjoys laughing in the company of his loved ones manages to lead a long life compared to those who suffer depression or have a negative outlook on life.

According to some studies, there is an association between the positive outlook and lower blood pressure. Individuals who have a positive mindset tend to have controlled blood pressure levels; whereas, those who look towards life in a negative perspective have the highest risk of developing high blood pressure. Moreover, positive individuals have the lower percentage of exposing themselves into evolving into cardiovascular disease.

Therefore, if you want to enjoy a quality life until your old age, it's time to recreate your mindset. You can always start with little things. In other words, you can marvel at the little things nature gives us like the sunlight, warmth, the sky or even the moon during the night.

Be conscious of your inner voice and how you talk to yourself. Avoid talking about your mistakes or highlighting your worries. Before you are tempted to do that, give yourself some space and assess the situation. While you can see unfavourable aspects, you always have the choice to shed on that matter. Don't forget to laugh in every chance you have. A good one can help lessen your mental burden, even making it easier for you to handle challenging problems.

Chapter 8: How Meditation Can Help in Lowering High Blood Pressure

In addition to the conventional methods of combating high blood pressure, Mindfulness-Based Reduction Technique (MBRS) is gaining followers and practitioners all over the world. By incorporating mindfulness meditation into your lifestyle along with physical fitness activity and weight management, your goal of reducing high blood pressure is achieved and thereby reverse its effect on your body.

According to a research study, to curb blood pressure and ward off hypertension, it is critical to keep your mind away from stress and anxiety.

Researchers from Case Western University School of Medicine conducted a study on hundred of patients with hypertension aging 30-60 years old. The program consisted of 8 sessions covering 2 ½ hours each. Participants were then asked to meditate using the body scan exercise for 45 minutes in six days per week. The study resulted in a significant outcome with the result indicating a 1.9-mm Hg decrease in diastolic blood pressure (DBP) and 4.8-mm Hg decrease in systolic blood pressure (SBP). The findings were published in the Psychosomatic Medicine Journal.

In a recent study on blood pressure, distress and coping, it was revealed that through a selected mind-body intervention, a decrease in blood pressure was detected relative to increased coping and decreased psychological distress in young adults conducive to high blood pressure.

Based on these studies, it was proven that meditation could be useful in lowering the level of blood pressure while combating the ill effects of stress and anxiety in the human body.

As you resolve to shift to a healthier lifestyle choice, you must incorporate meditation into your everyday routine. Making a habit of practicing daily or doing meditation exercises even for just 20 minutes is sure to make a big difference on how your body moves, how your mind thinks, and how your body feels.

When your mind and emotions are calm and controllable, you're in a better position to face all the challenges in your life and the goals that you have set for yourself – which in this case happens to be regulating your blood pressure to a reasonable level.

Those negative feelings including worry, anxiety, and fear plus the regular occurrence of stress as you are regularly exposed to various stressors can be significantly relieved by a daily practice of meditation. As your mind is cleared of muddled thoughts, keeping you stuck in unhealthy behaviors, you will be surprised to see how you would see life in a different viewpoint. All the changes in your life always begin in your mind.

Your mind always has the power over your body – from the tip of your hair down to the tip of your toes. Being able to control your mind and tame it so you can lead it to where you want is an efficient way of calming your overall sense so as not to send your heart beating or pumping as it usually does. When you can do this, then you are getting rid of the stressors that tend to send your blood pressure up.

Rather than doing the same routine using the same mindset and results that are disappointing, meditation allows you to set the stages for some significant shift in your life, and this includes, primarily your health.

MANAGING YOUR HEALTH, SAVING YOUR LIFE!

Just as human illness is relatively stress-related, meditation works well to relieve you from stress. It likewise helps in treating illnesses. Not only mediation resolve the issue on high blood pressure or hypertension risks, but it is also associated with the relief of the following diseases:

- Skin disorders
- Mild depression
- Pre-menstrual syndrome and dysmenorrhea
- Sleeping apnea and fatigue
- Recurring pain including headaches

- Respiratory issues like asthma and emphysema

- Rheumatoid Arthritis (RA) symptoms

- Gastrointestinal distress

- Irritable bowel syndrome

Health and medical condition like the ones we have here will undoubtedly deprive you of the vitality and live a life of fun and enjoyment. When you let stress weight you down as you are burdened with anxiety and negative thoughts and emotions, it stresses that is in control and not you!

Could there be more satisfying than having a cure for a stress-related illness that is natural? This is what meditation is offering you – A life of happiness – free from the claw of this deadly sickness.

A Way To Do Your Meditation Exercise

To start, find a comfortable place to do your exercise. Though old-timers can do it anywhere and would find it easy to achieve their meditation goal anywhere and anytime, beginners can get easily distracted; hence, you need a more quiet and serene place to meditate. You can either sit on a chair or the floor as long as you feel comfortable and relaxed. If you need something to soothe your senses, prepare some music.

Start by closing your eyes or just focus your attention on something like maybe the floor near where you are sitting. Then start breathing in and out gently, trying to feel the air as it passes through your nostrils and runs through every part of your body before you slowly take it out through your mouth, Feel every moment – either you focus on your breathing, or you focus on the object of your attention.

If you are closing your eyes, imagine of something – an image, an object, a mantra or anything you want to connect with. If you find your mind wandering out of focus, slowly get it back to being focused without judging yourself. The goal here is to be able to control your thinking to focus on something and not get affected emotionally but just silently look at it at the present moment.

Focusing on your breathing gives you a new awareness of your life, and while you are doing this activity, you may be able to grasp a new meaning to your existence. This could be a simple and quite exercise that could last for a few minutes, but out of it, something new – an insight maybe will be revealed to you in a spur of a moment.

Short as it is, you could not imagine the benefits this meditation exercise can bring you – physically, mentally, emotionally, and spiritually. It is for this reason that more and more people resort back to transcendental or mindfulness meditation as a way of treating stress to reverse the effects of high blood pressure or minimize the risks of more severe health problems.

Ideally, set aside 15-30 minutes a day for meditation so calm down your senses and prepare them for facing the daily struggles and challenges in life. This way, your body won't feel threatened and set itself to a fight or flight mode which causes it to produce some hormonal change in your body, sending your heart to build more pressure and forcing the arterial wall to break.

There are some online resources and tools like the Insight CD System, which you can set up by yourself and so a quick meditation session for 20 minutes or more depending on your preference.

While listening to the CD, you can teach your brain to work n synchronization –that is, training your left and right side of the brain to work in consonance to create a comprehensive distribution of electrical activity and energy patterns throughout your mind instead of having it confined to limited areas. This tool is designed in agreement with the result of a study which indicates that this full brain synchronization is active at times of intense creativity, clarity, and inspiration.

To sum this up, whether you are doing meditation without the use of the Insight audio CD or any tool like this, make sure that that you incorporate the meditation exercise in your daily activities. Make this a habit, not only to regulate your high blood pressure but a part of a healthy lifestyle. It's a simple step, but its lasting result can have a profound and lasting effect on your overall physical health and mental wellbeing.

CONCLUSION

A significant number of hypertension sufferers are now getting tired of experiencing the debilitating effects of drug prescriptions and medication that most opted to resort back to the natural remedies. Now that many are asking if the natural way of treating high blood pressure works, proven studies answer this question with a big "YES!"

However, natural treatment is a holistic approach that needs to be consolidated into your lifestyle to be able to benefit from it entirely. It does not answer to only one area of your life but needs to make a thorough overhauling of your wellbeing.

Now that you have become aware of the extent that natural remedies can do to your goal of bringing down to the reasonable level your high blood pressure, you can use this knowledge to regulate your blood pressure and manage your hypertension to prevent the onset of other complications or more severe illnesses.

High blood pressure can be a silent killer only if you neglect to give enough attention to your lifestyle. It's not high blood that kills, but it's your failure to create a healthy lifestyle that can give you a better, safer, and longer life!

The next step is for you to [join our email newsletter](#) to receive updates on any upcoming new book releases or promotions. You can sign-up for free and as a bonus, you will also receive our "*7 Fitness Mistakes You Don't Know You're Making*" book! This bonus book breaks down many of the most common fitness mistakes and will demystify many of the complexities and science of getting into shape. Having all this fitness knowledge and science organized into an actionable step-by-step book will help you get started in the right direction in your fitness journey! To join our free email newsletter and grab your free book, please visit the link and signup: www.hmwpublishing.com/gift

Finally, if you enjoyed this book, then I would like to ask you for a favor, would you be kind enough to leave a review for this book? It would be greatly appreciated!

Thank you and good luck in your journey!

About the Co-Author

My name is George Kaplo; I'm a certified personal trainer from Montreal, Canada. I'll start off by saying I'm not the biggest guy you will ever meet and this has never really been my goal. In fact, I started working out to overcome my biggest insecurity when I was younger, which was my self-confidence. This was due to my height measuring only 5 foot 5 inches (168cm), it pushed me down to attempt anything I ever wanted to achieve in life. You may be going through some challenges right now, or you may simply want to get fit, and I can certainly relate.

For me personally, I was always kind of interested in the health & fitness world and wanted to gain some muscle due to the numerous bullying in my teenage years about my height and my overweight body. I figured I couldn't do anything about my height, but I sure can do something about how my body looked like. This was the beginning of my transformation journey. I had no idea where to start, but I just got started. I felt worried and afraid at times that other people would make fun of me for doing the exercises the wrong way. I always wished I had a friend that was next to me who was knowledgeable enough to help me get started and "show me the ropes."

After a lot of work, studying and countless trial and errors. Some people began to notice how I was getting more fit and how I was starting to form a keen interest in the topic. This led many friends and new faces to come to me and ask me for fitness advice. At first, it seemed odd when people asked me to help them get in shape. But what kept me going is when they started to see changes in their own body and told me it's the first time that they saw real results! From there, more people kept coming to me, and it made me realize after so much reading and studying in this field that it did help me but it also allowed me to help others. I'm now a fully certified personal trainer and have trained numerous clients to date who have achieved amazing results.

Today, my brother Alex Kaplo (also a Certified Personal Trainer) and I own & operate this publishing venture, where we bring passionate and expert authors to write about health and fitness topics. We also run an online fitness website "HelpMeWorkout.com" and I would love to connect with by inviting you to visit the website on the following page and signing up to our e-mail newsletter (you will even get a free book).

Last but not least, if you are in the position I was once in and you want some guidance, don't hesitate and ask... I'll be there to help you out!

Your friend and coach,

George Kaplo

Certified Personal Trainer

Download another book for Free

I want to thank you for purchasing this book and offer you another book (just as long and valuable as this book), "Health & Fitness Mistakes You Don't Know You're Making", completely free.

Visit the link below to signup and receive it:

www.hmwpublishing.com/gift

In this book, I will break down the most common health & fitness mistakes, you are probably committing right now, and I will reveal how you can easily get in the best shape of your life!

In addition to this valuable gift, you will also have an opportunity to get our new books for free, enter giveaways, and receive other valuable emails from me. Again, visit the link to sign up:

www.hmwpublishing.com/gift

Copyright 2017 by HMW Publishing - All Rights Reserved.

This document by HMW Publishing owned by the A&G Direct Inc company, is geared towards providing exact and reliable information in regards to the topic and issue covered. The publication is sold with the idea that the publisher is not required to render accounting, officially permitted, or otherwise, qualified services. If advice is necessary, legal or professional, a practiced individual in the profession should be ordered.

From a Declaration of Principles which was accepted and approved equally by a Committee of the American Bar Association and a Committee of Publishers and Associations.

In no way is it legal to reproduce, duplicate, or transmit any part of this document in either electronic means or in printed format. Recording of this publication is strictly prohibited, and any storage of this document is not allowed unless with written permission from the publisher. All rights reserved.

The information provided herein is stated to be truthful and consistent, in that any liability, in terms of inattention or otherwise, by any usage or abuse of any policies, processes, or directions contained within is the solitary and utter responsibility of the recipient reader. Under no circumstances will any legal responsibility or blame be held against the publisher for any reparation, damages, or monetary loss due to the information herein, either directly or indirectly.

The information herein is offered for informational purposes solely, and is universal as so. The presentation of the information is without contract or any type of guarantee assurance.

The trademarks that are used are without any consent, and the publication of the trademark is without permission or backing by the trademark owner. All trademarks and brands within this book are for clarifying purposes only and are the owned by the owners themselves, not affiliated with this document.

For more great books visit:

HMWPublishing.com

www.ingramcontent.com/pod-product-compliance
Lightning Source LLC
Chambersburg PA
CBHW071911070526
44583CB00016B/1945